© JOLLY JULY
BY SANDEEP RAVIDUTT SHARMA

Table of Contents

Foreword IV

JOLLY JULY..1

© JOLLY JULY
BY SANDEEP RAVIDUTT SHARMA

Foreword

This book provides you with a list of 100 motivational quotes and thoughts about LIFE, churned out by my mind with the consciousness, grace and energy of Shiva Shakti. I'm sure if you keep reading, referring, sharing these thoughts and quotes about LIFE, you may derive inspiration and develop good understanding of various perspectives and facts. Stay positive and fearless of the outcome while you perform. Trust your knowledge but remember to give your best always. Welcome the change or be the change.

"Your positive thoughts can weave a Jolly good day for you and the world."

I sincerely hope, you will find this book amazing, interesting, rejuvenating, unique and a constant source of inspiration.

Thank You and Happy Reading.

JOLLY JULY

© **JOLLY JULY**
BY SANDEEP RAVIDUTT SHARMA

Your Smile can please everyone without uttering a single word.

© JOLLY JULY
BY SANDEEP RAVIDUTT SHARMA

© Copyright 2018 Sandeep Ravidutt Sharma - All rights reserved.

In no way is it legal to reproduce, duplicate, or transmit any part of this document in either electronic means or in printed format. Recording of this publication is strictly prohibited and any storage of this document is not allowed unless with written permission from the publisher. All rights reserved. The information provided herein is stated to be truthful and consistent, in that any liability, in terms of inattention or otherwise, by any usage or abuse of any policies, processes, or directions contained within is the solitary and utter responsibility of the recipient reader. Under no circumstances will any legal responsibility or blame be held against the author / publisher for any reparation, damages, or monetary loss due to the information herein, either directly or indirectly. The author own all copyrights.

Legal Notice:
This book is copyright protected. This is only for personal use. You cannot amend, distribute, sell, use, quote or paraphrase any part or the content within this book without the consent of the author or copyright owner. Legal action will be pursued if this is breached.

Disclaimer Notice:
Please note the information contained within this book is for motivational, educational and knowledge sharing purpose only. Every attempt has been made to provide the reader accurate, up to date and reliable complete information. No warranties of any kind are expressed or implied. Readers acknowledge that the author is not engaging in the rendering of legal, financial, medical or professional advice. By reading this document, the reader agrees that under no circumstances the author / publisher is responsible for any losses, direct or indirect, which are incurred as a result of the use of information contained within this document, including, but not limited to, —errors, omissions, or inaccuracies.

If you have further questions, contact on **Tel: +919969256731**
Email: sandeepraviduttsharma@gmail.com

© **JOLLY JULY**
BY SANDEEP RAVIDUTT SHARMA

Dedication

This book is dedicated to **Shiva Shakti** - the epitome of love. Lord Shiva is pure consciousness symbolising the masculine principle. Goddess Shakti symbolises the active feminine energy of Shiva and is synonymously identified with **Tripura Sundari, Sati** or **Parvati**.

These primal principles are also called as PURUSHA representing consciousness and PRAKRITI denoting the nature. Shiva and Shakti are manifestations of the all-in-one divine consciousness. Shiva is the paternal love of God that gives us consciousness, knowledge and clarity. Shakti is the motherly love of God that showers warmth, care and ensures our protection. Shiva and Shakti exist within each of us as the masculine and feminine energy. To please **Shiva Shakti** praying for the well being, love, happiness, strength, positive energy and success of my readers in their life, I hereby recite the following mantra...

"Sarva Mangala Mangalye Shive Sarvartha Sadhike Sharanye Tryambake Gauri Narayani Namostute"

© JOLLY JULY
BY SANDEEP RAVIDUTT SHARMA

Accept your imperfection better late than never.

© **JOLLY JULY**
BY SANDEEP RAVIDUTT SHARMA

Nothing seems right when you lose trust. Do enough to maintain trust.

© **JOLLY JULY**
BY SANDEEP RAVIDUTT SHARMA

Rise against exploitation in time or you lose the advantage to combat.

© **JOLLY JULY**
BY SANDEEP RAVIDUTT SHARMA

Actions are more trustworthy in place of your assurance.

© **JOLLY JULY**
BY SANDEEP RAVIDUTT SHARMA

Doing nothing and expecting something is just a dream. Even to dream you need to sleep.

© **JOLLY JULY**
BY SANDEEP RAVIDUTT SHARMA

Drop the junk of yesterday to pick up the flower of today.

© **JOLLY JULY**
BY SANDEEP RAVIDUTT SHARMA

Why plan to knock the door when its usually open. Just walk in with a cheerful attitude.

Live your own life even in poverty rather than live a borrowed life in richness.

© **JOLLY JULY**
BY SANDEEP RAVIDUTT SHARMA

Rock the world with your wonderful talent.

© **JOLLY JULY**
BY SANDEEP RAVIDUTT SHARMA

What made you laugh today may not do the same tomorrow. Everything changes with time.

The wonderful world exists only when we believe and feel it now.

Your attitude decides whether you will make friends or foes.

© **JOLLY JULY**
BY SANDEEP RAVIDUTT SHARMA

Sometimes it takes a lifetime to know self while many of us claim to know the world.

© **JOLLY JULY**
BY SANDEEP RAVIDUTT SHARMA

When your execution starts following the idea, you can win.

© JOLLY JULY
BY SANDEEP RAVIDUTT SHARMA

Instead of sitting in the darkness why not burn a candle of knowledge and convey the right message.

© **JOLLY JULY**
BY SANDEEP RAVIDUTT SHARMA

Your efforts walks with your mind, don't let your mind run and leave behind EFFORTS.

© **JOLLY JULY**
BY SANDEEP RAVIDUTT SHARMA

Nothing builds faster than friendship.

© **JOLLY JULY**
BY SANDEEP RAVIDUTT SHARMA

Write down your ideas, or it would fly out of your mind.

© **JOLLY JULY**
BY SANDEEP RAVIDUTT SHARMA

Tests are inevitable for those who are eyeing the Crown.

© JOLLY JULY
BY SANDEEP RAVIDUTT SHARMA

Track your progress by comparing your today with yesterday instead of trying to match with your neighbour.

© **JOLLY JULY**
BY SANDEEP RAVIDUTT SHARMA

Relationships blossom only when 'I' is replaced by 'We' and you enjoy togetherness.

© **JOLLY JULY**
BY SANDEEP RAVIDUTT SHARMA

Share your ideas if you can't execute on your own.

Don't beg or borrow happiness when you can create it with your sincere love and togetherness.

© JOLLY JULY
BY SANDEEP RAVIDUTT SHARMA

Don't resign but be eager and cheerful to sign up for a new role.

© **JOLLY JULY**
BY SANDEEP RAVIDUTT SHARMA

Remove greed from your mind today and you will know how kindness looks like.

© **JOLLY JULY**
BY SANDEEP RAVIDUTT SHARMA

The quality of your thoughts is very much influenced by what you learn and experience. At other times, your thoughts determine your experiences.

Many a times how you may think makes you either rich or poor.

© **JOLLY JULY**
BY SANDEEP RAVIDUTT SHARMA

Competition helps you to know your strengths and areas of concern.

© **JOLLY JULY**
BY SANDEEP RAVIDUTT SHARMA

Your talk doesn't make you a leader. It's your plan and action on the ground that creates one.

© **JOLLY JULY**
BY SANDEEP RAVIDUTT SHARMA

Love stays close to happiness. Embrace love and be happy.

© **JOLLY JULY**
BY SANDEEP RAVIDUTT SHARMA

The honest approach builds trust with others.

© JOLLY JULY
BY SANDEEP RAVIDUTT SHARMA

Those who believe in God, can feel his presence during joy or grief.

© **JOLLY JULY**
BY SANDEEP RAVIDUTT SHARMA

Experience doesn't guarantee the future win but is definitely an insurance against lessons learnt from past failures.

© **JOLLY JULY**
BY SANDEEP RAVIDUTT SHARMA

Not everyone may know about your changing moods. Give them sometime to understand.

© JOLLY JULY
BY SANDEEP RAVIDUTT SHARMA

Instead of signing a treaty for no first use of the deadly weapons why can't people in power sign treaty of friendship and peace.

© **JOLLY JULY**
BY SANDEEP RAVIDUTT SHARMA

Don't expect life to be a straight line. Get ready to travel on a zig zag path and surprise awaits you at every turn.

© **JOLLY JULY**
BY SANDEEP RAVIDUTT SHARMA

It's not always important to know whether you have won or lost but how did you play matters the most for a thinking soul?

© **JOLLY JULY**
BY SANDEEP RAVIDUTT SHARMA

Feeling great in life is fine but doing great is the best.

When goodness waves at you don't say goodbye instead open the door to welcome.

Don't let false ego start taking your decisions after you have won.

© **JOLLY JULY**
BY SANDEEP RAVIDUTT SHARMA

Check out on your strengths before you decide to challenge.

© **JOLLY JULY**
BY SANDEEP RAVIDUTT SHARMA

Look forward to meet surprise as you move on in life.

© **JOLLY JULY**
BY SANDEEP RAVIDUTT SHARMA

Work on your self for the good and see how it makes your life beautiful.

© **JOLLY JULY**
BY SANDEEP RAVIDUTT SHARMA

You feel happy when someone is listening.

© JOLLY JULY
BY SANDEEP RAVIDUTT SHARMA

Conquer your bitterness with words of forgiveness.

© JOLLY JULY
BY SANDEEP RAVIDUTT SHARMA

Strong visualisation comes from self-belief which ultimately makes you a winner.

© **JOLLY JULY**
BY SANDEEP RAVIDUTT SHARMA

Your goodwill can make you richer again. It's just a matter of time for the turnaround.

© **JOLLY JULY**
BY SANDEEP RAVIDUTT SHARMA

Don't assume things when you can get the facts.

© JOLLY JULY
BY SANDEEP RAVIDUTT SHARMA

The magic of love is felt when you are ready to receive and allow the other to express.

© JOLLY JULY
BY SANDEEP RAVIDUTT SHARMA

Question helps you to understand what is needed.

© JOLLY JULY
BY SANDEEP RAVIDUTT SHARMA

It's a lovely and jolly good day to start again in life.

© **JOLLY JULY**
BY SANDEEP RAVIDUTT SHARMA

Don't go too much into the future when you can't even accurately predict the next step forward.

When you give the gift of love, you never return empty handed but with riches of love back.

Push your efforts in the right direction if you intend to fulfill your dreams.

© **JOLLY JULY**
BY SANDEEP RAVIDUTT SHARMA

Never let the world fall on you. Get up and be brave enough to try again and rise in life.

© JOLLY JULY
BY SANDEEP RAVIDUTT SHARMA

Ignore the company of Greed and anger if you are looking for the address of peace and happiness.

© **JOLLY JULY**
BY SANDEEP RAVIDUTT SHARMA

Words lose its charm when they are thrown at you and not when you absorb them within.

© JOLLY JULY
BY SANDEEP RAVIDUTT SHARMA

Wonderful are the ways of the Lord. He makes you run through the darkness while ask the Sun to rise and show you the path soon.

© **JOLLY JULY**
BY SANDEEP RAVIDUTT SHARMA

Go for it when the opportunity knocks.

© JOLLY JULY
BY SANDEEP RAVIDUTT SHARMA

Pick up positive thoughts for the day that can motivate and drop fear forever.

© JOLLY JULY
BY SANDEEP RAVIDUTT SHARMA

It's easy to claim Impossible but it needs real efforts to make it possible.

© **JOLLY JULY**
BY SANDEEP RAVIDUTT SHARMA

Don't shout from your balcony when you can call and speak softly.

© **JOLLY JULY**
BY SANDEEP RAVIDUTT SHARMA

Swallow your pride if it can save someone's life.

© **JOLLY JULY**
BY SANDEEP RAVIDUTT SHARMA

Dare to speak against injustice and stop its march.

© **JOLLY JULY**
BY SANDEEP RAVIDUTT SHARMA

Curious questions help you to discover new ways.

© **JOLLY JULY**
BY SANDEEP RAVIDUTT SHARMA

Sincerity is enough to accept our limitations and showcase capabilities.

© **JOLLY JULY**
BY SANDEEP RAVIDUTT SHARMA

God makes the way for one and all. All you need is trust and patience.

© JOLLY JULY
BY SANDEEP RAVIDUTT SHARMA

Life can be like a hard rock. Those are brave enough and gifted with an innovative mind can play musical flute sitting on the hard rock enjoying the dip of the Sun in the Ocean aiming to relax and recharge again for the next Sun rise.

© **JOLLY JULY**
BY SANDEEP RAVIDUTT SHARMA

Don't be choosy when its time to give respect.

© JOLLY JULY
BY SANDEEP RAVIDUTT SHARMA

Seek attention when the matter is critical. Demand solution before it becomes critical.

© **JOLLY JULY**
BY SANDEEP RAVIDUTT SHARMA

Don't try to find logic in everything you experience. For ages we hardly know about our own self precisely.

© **JOLLY JULY**
BY SANDEEP RAVIDUTT SHARMA

Be ready to serve the humanity whether someone calls you or not.

© **JOLLY JULY**
BY SANDEEP RAVIDUTT SHARMA

Wishful thinking is good but action on the ground matters the most.

© **JOLLY JULY**
BY SANDEEP RAVIDUTT SHARMA

Let the hunger for knowledge grow, and learning becomes way of life.

© JOLLY JULY
BY SANDEEP RAVIDUTT SHARMA

Moments of joy come in everyone's life. Few of us make merry while others still live with doubt and lose them.

© **JOLLY JULY**
BY SANDEEP RAVIDUTT SHARMA

Moments of joy are short-lived for those who fail to live them now but are trying to savour for tomorrow.

© JOLLY JULY
BY SANDEEP RAVIDUTT SHARMA

The outburst of anger can't stand against humbleness.

© **JOLLY JULY**
BY SANDEEP RAVIDUTT SHARMA

Let the world know about your noble intention of planting the seeds now for tomorrow's shade.

© **JOLLY JULY**
BY SANDEEP RAVIDUTT SHARMA

Promise your own self to stay positive before you commit the world.

© **JOLLY JULY**
BY SANDEEP RAVIDUTT SHARMA

Connect with people, and you never know who learns from you or teaches you newer things about dear life.

© JOLLY JULY
BY SANDEEP RAVIDUTT SHARMA

You can't grow big by ridiculing the other.

© JOLLY JULY
BY SANDEEP RAVIDUTT SHARMA

When you can't convince others about your capabilities, it's better to simply perform.

Challenges like your response.

© JOLLY JULY
BY SANDEEP RAVIDUTT SHARMA

Pursue your dream with a smile on your face.

© **JOLLY JULY**
BY SANDEEP RAVIDUTT SHARMA

Beautiful ideas come from joyful mind.

© JOLLY JULY
BY SANDEEP RAVIDUTT SHARMA

When life makes you laugh, don't try to find the reason.

© **JOLLY JULY**
BY SANDEEP RAVIDUTT SHARMA

Life is a journey from darkness towards light.

© JOLLY JULY
BY SANDEEP RAVIDUTT SHARMA

Doubting other is quite easy but to trust someone needs constant efforts, positive attitude and lots of patience.

© JOLLY JULY
BY SANDEEP RAVIDUTT SHARMA

Fast tracking your watch you can't reach your destination early.

© **JOLLY JULY**
BY SANDEEP RAVIDUTT SHARMA

Insist on the agenda before you decide to meet.

© **JOLLY JULY**
BY SANDEEP RAVIDUTT SHARMA

Come out of your comfort zone if you really want to grow and discover the world.

© **JOLLY JULY**
BY SANDEEP RAVIDUTT SHARMA

As you move towards excellence, SUCCESS keeps following you.

© JOLLY JULY
BY SANDEEP RAVIDUTT SHARMA

It's better to lose your wealth rather than your mind.

© JOLLY JULY
BY SANDEEP RAVIDUTT SHARMA

There may be hundred of ways to present something, choosing the best one reflects your personality.

© JOLLY JULY
BY SANDEEP RAVIDUTT SHARMA

Always believe and make efforts to ensure that you are the best but at the same time don't assume others to be the worst.

As you start understanding the pain and suffering of others, you will soon realise how better you are.

© JOLLY JULY
BY SANDEEP RAVIDUTT SHARMA

Joyful living starts with feeling content with whatever you have got.

© JOLLY JULY
BY SANDEEP RAVIDUTT SHARMA

Walk alone if you need to watch the world without getting influenced by others.

© JOLLY JULY
BY SANDEEP RAVIDUTT SHARMA

With colours of joy you can paint the rainbow of happiness.

www.ingramcontent.com/pod-product-compliance
Lightning Source LLC
Chambersburg PA
CBHW031439210526
45464CB00005B/2271